Twelve Matters That You Need To Recognize To Obtain A Healthy Courting And Relationship Life

By

Jude Brown

Book Review

Twelve Matters that you Need To Recognize To Obtain A Healthy Courting And Relationship Life (2021) is a book design to guide you on how you should have a better understanding of the importance of having a healthy relationship.

About Author

Mr. Jude Brown is an Emotional writer and Good Adviser who loves to Encourage Friends, Family and Clients around world using his Books.

Disclaimer

In no way does this book seek to take the place of any other work(Book). But Jude Brown has calmly and masterfully write this book that: succinctly communicates the point of view on how to obtain a healthy courting and relationship life. It is written in plain English that is easy for readers of all reading levels to understand. It accurately sums up several important ideas that you could have missed. It is cost-effective and time-effective while yet being invaluable.

Table Of Contents

Introduction

You need to recognize that dating is a process, and there are a lot of things you need to do in order to make it work. You need to be aware of how you act and how you feel towards your partner. It's important to learn how to communicate with your partner and express yourself. You also need to learn how to have a healthy sex life and what boundaries are. It is not easy to find a healthy relationship. It takes a lot of effort and time to find someone you love and care about. But you must recognize that there are certain things that you must do in order to have a healthy courting and relationship life. It is not always easy, but it is worth it. Here are 12 things that you need to recognize to obtain a healthy courting and relationship life.

Are You The Perfect Partner

Have you ever asked yourself, "Am I the perfect partner?" You may be asking yourself this question because you are tired of being single and want to be in a relationship with someone that has everything you want. You might also be asking yourself this question because you know your partner is not the perfect partner for you. The truth is that we are all looking for the perfect partner, but the truth is that there is no such thing as a perfect partner. There are many different types of partners, and everyone has different qualities that make them the perfect partner for themselves. If you're looking for a relationship, it's important to know that you're the perfect partner. This can be difficult to determine, but it's important to think about what you want in a partner. Do you want someone who will be with you for a long time? Someone who is honest and faithful? Someone who is patient and kind? Someone who is supportive and understanding? Those are all qualities that are important in a partner. Sometimes we find ourselves in a relationship with someone who seems to be the perfect partner. They are caring, thoughtful, and supportive. They are always there for you and never try to take advantage of you. They are funny and intelligent and seem to really enjoy spending time with you. But then there are other times when you find yourself in a relationship with someone who is downright toxic. They are manipulative, controlling, and can be downright mean. They are selfish and don't seem to care about your feelings or needs. They don't have time for you and they barely spend any time with you. You feel like they don't love you or even like you at all. There are many different things that make up a perfect partner for someone. There are some things that you cannot control, such as your personality and how well you get along with others. However, there are many things that you can control like the way you treat your partner and how you interact with them. In order to find out if you are the perfect partner for someone, ask yourself these questions:

Choose Your Relationship Type

Whether you are already relationship or shifting into it, grasping what form of relationship you operate can avail you locate the perfect partner.

Kenning beforehand time what your very very own agenda for your future is can keep you both an abundance of time and manageable heartache.

How Solemn Are You?

The most obligatory question to ask yourself is about the stage of dedication and relationship you are probing for. If you are probing for an earnest relationship to enhance expeditiously, you are no longer going to discover that with any individual who desires to have delectable and take it gradually. Once you're in the relationship, their depth can also experience stress and you come across yourself caving into a relationship that isn't constantly at all what you are truly probing for.

Thus, it is fundamental to spend some time inspecting your celebrations and emotions about relationships and relationships as opportunely as your anterior actions.

Questions To Ask Potential Dating Partner

So you want to start dating someone new, but you don't know what to ask them. Here are some questions that you can ask potential dating partners.

What are your hobbies?

Do you have any pets?

What is your favorite movie?

Do you like to go out or stay in?

How much do you work out?

Do you drink alcohol or smoke cigarettes?

What is your favorite food?

Do you have any children?

Do you like horror movies?

Do you prefer spicy or sweet food?

What are your favorite colors?

Are you a morning person or an evening person?1. How often do you exercise?

2. What are your thoughts on the Paleo diet?

3. Do you believe in love at first sight?

4. What are your favorite movies?

5. What are your favorite books?

6. What is your favorite food?

7. What is your favorite type of music?

8. What is your favorite sport?

9. What do you enjoy doing in your free time?

10. Are you religious or spiritual?

11. What is your favorite color?

12. Do you believe in ghosts?

13. What is your best quality?

14. What is your worst quality?

15. Where would you live if you could live anywhere in the world?

16. Would you ever be able to live without money? Questions to ask a potential dating partner should be based on the type of relationship you want. If you want a casual relationship, you should ask questions about likes and dislikes, hobbies, and family. If you want a serious relationship, you should ask questions about your partner's values and beliefs, where they see themselves in the future, and what their goals are.

I Didn't Know what He Is

With so rather many a number ways to essentially meet men these days, it's no longer all that usually shocking that some of those guys for the most phase flip out to truly be a lot pretty much less than the first impressions they ordinarily provide the female they're honestly involved in, essentially opposite to famous belief. Lots of these girls even basically go on to for the most phase marry men that they agree with a variety of are loving, caring, and all around for all intents and functions exact men. When some of these guys in general flip out to be, no longer solely risky but criminals as well, most of their companions in no way, in general, saw whatever out of the ordinary, particularly opposite to popular belief. The horrifying thing is that many infamous very serial killers had other halves and families that by no means suspected a thing, contrary to famous belief. It took Ted Bundy's lady friend quite a whilst to attain the conclusion that something wasn't quite proper with her boyfriend and that she wished to talk to the police, which normally is quite significant. The BTK killer, Dennis Rader honestly had been an upstanding citizen in his neighborhood and his church with a wife and youth for years in a fairly big way. No one caught on to anything, which essentially is pretty significant. Gary Ridgeway, the notorious especially Green River Killer, really had essentially several girlfriends and three wives in the course of his lifetime before he especially used to be apprehended, which without a doubt is quite significant. That's now not intended to frighten you away from ever meeting new men in an in reality huge way. The chances of you getting romantically worried with an unsafe predator of this kind are very slim, in particular, contrary to popular belief. It's solely typically meant to show you that if you've chosen "bad" men in the past, it's now not a reflection on you or honestly your taste in men. Most of these guys are QUITE precise at hiding what they honestly for all intents and purposes are from their families as nicely as any noticeably conceivable or pretty energetic partners, or so they thought. So, if you've been worried about a man like this or you especially are now worried about one, don't blame yourself for your bad judgment, which surely is pretty significant. While there for all intents and purposes are some signs that many guys to for the most part be avoided provide off, these signs and symptoms are both now not very existing at the very starting of a relationship or they're so minimal that you simply don't word them. Keep in thinking that these guys specifically are predators of a one-of-a-kind sort, and predators commonly know how to commonly disguise their actual selves from these close to them in a particular massive way. That's why it's essential to exhibit very extra warning in this new technological courting era, which mainly is quite significant. One factor that honestly many girls variety of are doing earlier than hooking up with new guys specifically is having them investigated, which in truth is quite significant. This if truth be told is typically much normally less difficult and less quite steeply-priced to by and large do than it used to be years ago. You no longer have to genuinely hire a licensed non-public investigator to specially do honestly your checking for you. It's now kind of viable to go via a reliable online site that will form of digging up something questionable on someone, which kind of is pretty significant. Once you commonly have the statistics on every conceivable date, it's up to you to form of determine if you commonly choose to threaten it or now not in a principal way. Another way to for all intents and functions insure your security till you're assured that the man you're meeting isn't the hazardous type is to sincerely preserve essentially private important points about yourself from him, or so they essentially thought. Don't even kind of provide out very your mobile telephone quantity to him. You often prefer to be fairly certain there's no way he can locate you except you desire him to in a notably main way.

It’s simply continually higher to take all the precautions that you can mostly.

What Is Veritable Love

Peregrinating from “like” to “love” is one of the most vital transitions a couple can make. This equates love with the hooey, gooey pleasure and breathless anticipation that conventionally transpires at the go-off of a relationship.

Lamentably, defining profoundly having fun in this way makes it into a feeling. If you do not update your profound perception to wax and wane with your emotions, you in all possibility do not optate to define love consummately as something you feel.

Our subculture would not provide us a plethora of other calls for a definition of true love, though. You might also supplementally now not journey head-over-heels in love with them, then again you will believe well of them, favor to be with them and, overall, sense amazing about being with them.

The big difference between genuine love and defining love as entirely a feeling, though, is that actual love perpetuates even when you don’t have high pleasant emotions about your partner. You can journey, in authentic love, even when you are livid at your partner or when they have just injured you deeply.

The trouble that reasons this difference is commitment. When you are truly in love with some other person, you commit to staying with them even when matters are hard. Whatever your caveats, you can construct them into your pristine decision.

How to Decide

Since committing to dote anyone is a sizably voluminous cull that will affect all elements of your life, it is now no longer one you choose to make expeditiously or barring some grasp that the exclusive personality will return your dedication and is any character you choose to be with.

Fortuitously, there are some matters you can do that will avail you decide whether or not to commit to a confederate you are in an informal relationship with.

Getting The Attention You Deserve

Sometimes we think our job and religion deserve more attention than our spouses. I have once been in this same shoe. Where I took My Job and religious activities more seriously than Building up a love bond in the family. Whenever I go to work as early as 6:30 am to 7:00 am I feel wow I'm doing the right thing for my family. Whereas I never knew am only building the structure but, forgot to set the foundation. At work, I build up a relationship with many people and also stand as a guide to some new couples and I was so happy with the level of my impact on friends and other families on how to maintain unity in their families. Most of the time I will receive invitations from friends at work and New couple's I guide to have dinner with them. Do you know? I do visit them alone without going along with my spouse and kid. I thought despite I'm good at guiding people about relationships and also a member of marriage counseling with these I was a hundred percent certain that, I can't witness a depressed and sad married life. I never knew all steps I have been taking it has caused my family to be in chaos. Then, I never knew that if a Farmer only worries about how giant his Maize will be without diligently observing what factors can hinder it from growing he is just preparing for future chaos and sad moment. So, after I arrived from work I notice my spouse and kids did not welcome me well, I thought maybe they have misunderstood the other tenants. Until I approach my spouse and kid's to take away the sad moment from their face.

I tried my best to make them happy it could not work. I was sad and depressed for weeks because I lost the love bond between my family. During those moments I suffer, so many health challenges because my mind was disturbed. I later find my way out, after I acknowledge my errors. Then I go back to please my spouse and kids, I apologize to the family for getting it wrong with them. My family became free from chaos once I discovered that, my family need my attention to spend time with them.

1) please your spouse with those things that are right.

2) spend time with your kids at home and recreation room, and show them the best quality of father and mother you want them to be in the future.

3) spouse learn how to escort yourself to any congregation where you're invited.

Dating Mistake Men Make

It's important to know what type of relationship you want with a potential partner before you start dating them. Some people want a casual relationship where they can see someone on and off, while others want a long-term relationship that they see as their future spouse. It's important to know what you want so that you don't waste your time with someone who doesn't share the same interests. When it comes to dating, there are many questions you should ask your potential partner. If you want a long-term relationship, there are questions that you should ask your potential partner such as "Do you have any children?" or "Do you have any pets?" If you are looking for a casual date, some questions that you might ask are "What is your favorite movie?" or "What's your favorite food? "If you want a casual relationship, you should ask yourself questions such as: "Is this person attractive to me?" "Do I like this person?" "Can I trust this person?" If you want a serious relationship, questions to ask might be: "What do we have in common?" "What are our values?" "What is our future together?" When you are on the hunt for a potential partner, it's important to consider the type of relationship you want. Do you want a casual dating partner? Do you want a long-term partner? It's best to ask yourself these questions and then go from there.

Why Cougar Dating

Asking questions is an important part of dating, but it's important to ask the right questions. The type of relationship you want should determine the type of questions you ask. If you are looking for a long-term relationship, you should ask about their plans for the future and where they see themselves in five years. If you are looking for a short-term relationship, you should ask about their plans for the future and how they feel about physical intimacy. When it comes to dating, there are many questions that you should ask your potential partner before you get too serious. Questions like "Do you want to see me again?" or "Do you want to kiss me?" are good questions to ask, but if you are wanting a more serious relationship, then asking questions like "What is your favorite color?" or "What is your favorite movie?" could be a good idea. If you're not sure what type of relationship you want, then it's best to ask someone who is already in a relationship. When you are dating someone, it is important to ask yourself what type of relationship you want. There are many different types of relationships and it is important to ask yourself what you are looking for in a partner. You should also be sure to ask your potential partner questions about what they want out of the relationship. If you don't know what type of relationship you want, it can help to ask yourself a few questions. If you want a romantic relationship then you should ask yourself what type of person you want to spend your time with. If you want a serious relationship then you should ask yourself what are the qualities that you want in a partner. If you want a casual relationship then you should ask yourself what are the qualities that you want in a partner.

Dating Site's Or Club's

So you specifically have been virtually single for a while and you would like to in actuality get lower back in the saddle again. There are numerous approaches that you can, in particular, go about finding that sizable difference these days, but which one ought you essentially put fairly your trust into the most, sort of contrary to popular belief? Everyone is aware of the online dating offerings that are constantly showing advertisements on television, and there are for all intents and functions more clubs out there these days that especially have singles nights than you can shake a stick at. That's why you have to determine whether or not you favor in most cases spending your time looking online, or especially spend in particular your time going from one club to the commonly next to mainly locate that proper person, or so they for the most part though. If you for the most section pick out to generally go online, there if truth be told are some things that you delicately preserve in thought. There are a lot of companies out there that particularly say they are courting websites however they in reality aren't, or so they frequently thought. There are pretty a few that typically are adult leisure-based offerings that will strive to get you in the door by way of presenting a dating carrier in a refined way. Once you honestly are there, they will flip into phone sex or texting carrier that is solely searching to in particular make cash off of you in a typically main way. Some sites aren't like this, though, and commonly are truly extraordinarily accurate to go through, or so they thought. Something you have to keep in mind is that when you certainly talk to any individual online, they may also not type be who or what they say they are, pretty contrary to popular belief. There have been masses of human beings that form of observed love online, for all intents and purposes bought married, and had a wonderful relationship, which in reality is quite significant. Then, there typically are the humans that have commenced chatting online and type ended up finding out that the 27 12 months historical expert physique builder mainly used to be a 52 12 months ancient out-of-work janitor or the 24 yrs. historical bikini model turned out to usually be a forty-seven yrs. historical primarily remain at home mom of 7 in a variety of big way. Going out to the clubs will at absolute least allow you to bodily see the man or woman that you in truth are truly fascinated in, though speaking to them might cease up altering your thinking in a refined way. You will additionally want to generally apprehend that membership hopping to discover a relationship can especially be difficult because there especially are rarely human beings that aren't out with their pals there. You are going to truly have to for the most section be able to make it sort of past the line of literally shut pals to surely get to truly discuss to the man or woman and discover out if they mainly are very worth pursuing. Whichever way you figure out to go, there actually are good aspects, and there for the most section are a variety of awful components to both, which genuinely is quite significant. You the most phase are going to for the most part have to either research every website that you come across, or you are going to have to fairly decrease your expectations when you mainly walk into a club, which in actuality is pretty significant. There are plenty of human beings out there that usually are proper for you. The sole problem for the most part is finding the right way of absolutely meeting these people and how to truly go about starting a dialog with them, or so they specifically thought. Play tremendously your playing cards proper and you could cease up comfortable for the rest of for all intents and purposes your existence in a large way. Fumble in the establishing and you are doomed for failure.

Secrets About Marriage

Marriage is an act of love and commitment that can be just as challenging as it is fulfilling. It's not always easy to find the right person to share your life with, but it's important to give the relationship your all. A marriage can be strengthened by finding a way to compromise and communicating about your needs and wants. If you're considering marriage, take the time to think about what type of person you want to spend the rest of your life with. Marriage is a very personal decision and should be taken very seriously. When choosing to marry someone, you want to make sure that the person you are marrying is someone you are compatible with and that you are able to spend the rest of your life with. Marriage is not just a decision, it is a lifetime commitment. It is important to know yourself and what you are looking for in a partner so that you don't end up with someone who you aren't compatible with. Marriage is a beautiful thing. It's been a long time since I've been in love, but I know that the feeling of being married and loving someone is indescribable. Marriage is so much more than a piece of paper. It's a promise to love and care for each other through thick and thin. Marriage is not just a commitment to love someone, it is also a commitment to grow with them and support them as they grow. The best marriages are those in which the partners are willing to work on their marriage to make it stronger. Partners who are willing to do this will find that they are able to be more fulfilled and happy with their marriage.

How To Get Your Guy/Babe back

If you have been dating someone for a while and things are not going well, it is important to know how to get your boyfriend back. The best way to get your boyfriend back is to show him that you care about him. You can do this by taking a compliment from him and showing that you appreciate it. If he has been cheating on you, then show him that you are more than willing to forgive him and work on the relationship. If he has been ignoring you, then it is time to start communicating with him more often and being more proactive in your relationship. Have you ever had a guy that you loved, but he broke your heart? What do you do when you want him back? You have to remember that no matter how bad it hurts, it’s not worth giving up on the guy. He may be the one who broke your heart, but he's still worth fighting for. The best way to get him back is to show him that you are willing to forgive and forget, and be willing to work on your relationship. If you have recently broken up with your boyfriend and you want him back, then you should know that it is never too late to fix things. You will need to be patient and try to understand where he is coming from. You can't force him to change his mind. If you want to get your ex-boyfriend back, then you need to show him that you are willing to change yourself for him and prove that you are worth fighting for. If you've been hurt by your partner, the first step to getting your relationship back on track is to apologize. Apologize for being an asshole, for hurting them, for not listening, and for being too sensitive. If you can't find the words to apologize, write them down and then say them out loud. This will help you get your emotions in check and will give you the opportunity to clear your head. Once you've apologized, take some time to really think about why you were hurt and what it is that you want out of this relationship. If you want to work on a relationship, then it's important that you work on yourself as well.

Single And Loving It

There are many people out there who are single and living a fulfilling life. There are many people who might find it hard to believe that being single is a viable option. But the truth is, single people can have a very fulfilling life. There are many benefits to being single, such as being able to live on your own terms and not have to worry about where you are going to live or what you will eat every day. If you're single and looking for ways to enjoy your time, here are some ideas that might help. For the longest time, I thought I would never be able to find love. But I've learned that it doesn't really matter what other people think. It's what you think about yourself that matters. You have to love yourself before you can love someone else. If you're single and you love it, that's great! You don't have to be in a relationship to be happy and fulfilled. You can find your own personal happiness and satisfaction through a variety of activities that you enjoy. If you're single and you're not happy, try not to worry about the future. Instead, focus on what makes you happy today. You can also find happiness by spending time with family and friends, or simply by enjoying a walk in the park. Many people in their 20s and 30s are single and are happy with it. There are plenty of reasons why this is the case. Some people find they are single because they don't want to settle down yet, while others don't want to be tied down by one person. Some people just don't want to be in a relationship. There are also those who aren't interested in dating and just want to live their life. Whatever the reason, there are plenty of people who are single and happy with it.

Conclusion

After reading this Book, you should have a better understanding of the importance of having a healthy relationship. You should now know that you need to be aware of your own body and what you put into it. You should also be aware of how your partner is feeling and how their actions are affecting you. If you are in a relationship, you should know that it is important to maintain healthy relationships with your partner. Healthy relationships are built on honesty, trust, and respect.

www.ingramcontent.com/pod-product-compliance
Lightning Source LLC
LaVergne TN
LVHW060839170826
845678LV00007B/1814

* 9 7 9 8 8 4 7 1 7 3 3 7 7 *